CONTENTS

INTRODUCTION:

What would you think if your children went to a school where experiences like these made them excited about learning?

In elementary school...

Students learn from their teacher that a nearby zoo will soon be getting some new animals. In a live video conference, a zoo staff member asks students to help design habitats for the animals. Students decide which animals they would like to focus on and work in teams to do research. Then they create drawings and scale models of the habitats. They stay in contact with zoo staff members, who help them gain the scientific knowledge they need to learn. The teacher also gives lessons and resources to guide the students. For a big finish, the students present their proposals to the zoo staff. In addition to learning science, these students are building skills in problem-solving, working in teams, making a presentation, and using technology.

In middle school ...

Taught by their English and history teachers teaming together, students learn what it means to be resilient—to be strong in the face of challenges. They read stories and study resilient heroes in the Civil Rights Movement in American history. Then they find members of their community today to interview—people who showed strength during challenges in their lives. Finally, the students write spoken-word poetry about how they can be resilient in their own lives. They perform their poetry at a community celebration, which they planned themselves. In addition to learning history, reading, and writing, these students are building skills in communicating with others, working in teams, and organizing an event.

In high school …

In their science class, students partner with a nonprofit organization working in Haiti to design and build solar ovens, using simple, low-cost materials. They develop various designs for the ovens, share them with engineers for feedback, and then improve them. Finally, they write reports, document their lab tests, and "pitch" their oven designs in a presentation to the engineers. The designs are also sent to the nonprofit organization for consideration for more testing. In addition to learning math and science, these students are building skills in "design thinking," working in teams, problem-solving, making a presentation, and creativity and innovation.

1. Carrer

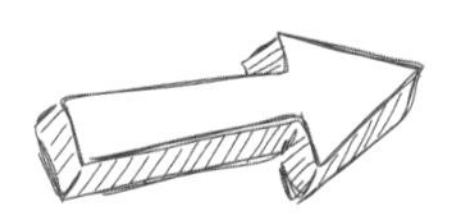

READ ON TO FIND OUT WHY STUDENTS NEED THESE KINDS OF EXPERIENCES, AND HOW THEY CAN GET THEM WHEN TEACHERS AND SCHOOLS USE PROJECT BASED LEARNING.
FOR MORE EXAMPLES OF PROJECTS, SEE PAGE 33..

THIS IS PROJECT BASED LEARNING

These are all real examples of Project Based Learning, or PBL. Because PBL has many benefits, it is becoming a more common practice in 21st century K–12 education. And as with any other teaching method, its success depends not only on the work of administrators and teachers but also on the understanding and support of parents and other community members.

This booklet is meant for parents and other members of the school community. It explains the “what” and the “why” of this teaching method, answering many questions people often have about PBL. In addition to reading this booklet, we also encourage you to talk with teachers and school leaders for more information about PBL at your school.

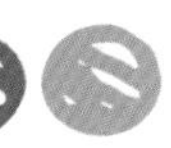

"I LOVE PBL BECAUSE IT'S LIKE A SECRET. THERE'S SO MUCH LEARNING BUT YOU DON'T REALIZE IT. THE TEACHERS HELP US BUT STUDENTS DO MOST OF THE THINKING. SOMETIMES, WE THINK SO MUCH THAT OUR HEADS HURT.

-- MADISON, 4TH GRADER,
NOVI, MICHIGAN

PART ONE:
WHY DO TODAY'S STUDENTS NEED PROJECT BASED LEARNING?

MORE AND MORE SCHOOLS TODAY ARE USING THE TEACHING METHOD OF PROJECT BASED LEARNING. THEY ARE MAKING THIS CHOICE FOR TWO REASONS:

- When school is more exciting, students learn better.
- When school teaches students more than basic information and skills, they are better prepared for their future.

Why aren't students excited by school?
Sometimes students find an assignment interesting, and some teachers are naturally good at engaging their students in learning. But much of the time in school, students are bored. Sometimes their heads might be in it, but often their hearts are not.

49% of American high school students say they are bored in at least one class every day. Another 17% say they are bored in every class, every day. - High School Survey of Student Engagement.

Much of the time in school, students do not learn actively. Instead, they fill out worksheets, read textbooks, and listen to the teacher talk. They memorize a lot of information, but they don't see a connection between this schoolwork and real life. Even students who get good grades often admit that they don't care very deeply about what they're doing in school.

But hasn't school always been boring?

The world today is different from how it used to be, and young people are different too. In the 21st century, students are less willing to just sit and listen to a teacher. They were raised in a world of technology and media, with new ways to get information. They like to use tech tools and social media to create things and work together. Young people are also hungry for learning that they find meaningful. They want to see the real-life or personal relevance of what they are taught in school. They want to make a contribution to their communities and world.

-- high school student

HOW ABOUT YOU

Even though those of us who are now adults did the work and graduated, many of us thought school was boring. But do you remember doing an interesting assignment at least once in a while? Wouldn't it be great if your child could do work like that regularly?

Don't students just have to learn things in school in case they need to know them later?

Students are often told, "Learn this because you'll need it later." That's not very motivating for most kids. If they need to know something now because it will help them do work they care about, they're more motivated to learn it. That's what happens in Project Based Learning. If students just memorize information for a test, they don't remember very much of it a year or a month or even just a week later. Students remember what they learn better when they use it, as they do in a project.

Think about a time when you learned something really well. Did you just memorize the information, or did you actually have to do something with what you learned?

What should students be taught in school so they can be successful in a job/career, or in college?

In the past, most students needed to learn only the basics of reading, writing, and arithmetic to be prepared for further education and life after school. A little knowledge of history and government and an appreciation for literature didn't hurt. But in today's information-age, high-tech economy, people need to know more than just basic facts in order to succeed.

Many jobs today require knowing how to use technology, solve complex problems, and work in an effective team. Many jobs require people to be "project managers," who know how to analyze a problem, figure out what needs to be done, and then get it done. And since many jobs in the United States are being lost today due to automation and outsourcing, it pays to be flexible and able to learn new skills. Creativity and entrepreneurship skills can help people succeed in a changing economy. Project Based Learning teaches all these things, along with the basics.

-- Joydip, parent of high school student, San Mateo, CA

Students who earn good grades and get high test scores can "play the game" of school, but can they lead a team, adapt to new situations, and "think out of the box" to solve real-life problems? That's what will help them succeed in an increasingly competitive workforce.

-- Jack, A.P. Physics student, Bellevue, WA

WHAT DO EMPLOYERS WANT WHEN THEY HIRE SOMEONE?

According to recent studies, employers say they value people who can:

- think critically and solve problems
- work well in teams
- communicate effectively
- take initiative and be responsible
- learn new skills when needed
- innovate and be creative
- manage their work independently

Project Based Learning gives students opportunities to learn these things.

What will help students succeed in college or technical schools?

Colleges and technical schools want students with the same kinds of skills employers want. They still expect students to have a sound base of academic knowledge, but they don't want students who only know a lot of information—or how to memorize it. They want students who understand more deeply and can apply what they know to the real world.

Learning in college still means attending lectures by professors, but that's not all. More and more colleges are moving away from a lectures-only approach. College students will also be asked to solve problems and work independently. Colleges want students who can work in teams, manage projects, and make presentations. Project Based Learning emphasizes all these skills.

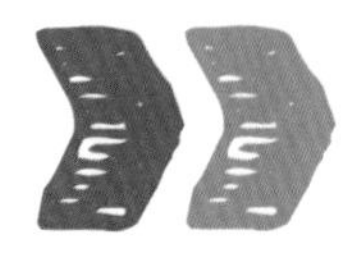

While working on a project in high school, students will still do some of their learning through traditional teaching tools such as lectures and tests. Students working on a project can still practice skills such as listening, note-taking, and memorizing information.

-- Leah, 4th grader, commenting on a project, Glen Burnie, MD

PART TWO:
WHAT IS PROJECT BASED LEARNING? HOW EFFECTIVE IS IT?

WHAT PBL IS AND IS NOT

Project Based Learning, or PBL, is a teaching method that engages students actively in learning by asking them to investigate an interesting and complex question, problem, or challenge, and then to create something in response. Projects can vary in length; some may take a week or two, others a month or more. Projects may be done individually, in teams, or by a whole class.

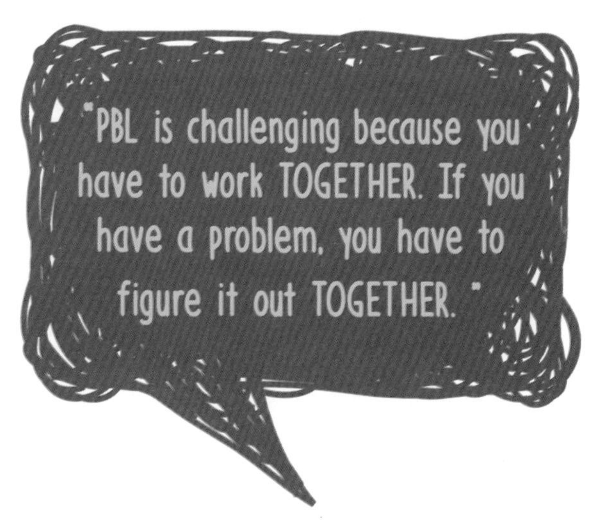

-- Aiden, 1st grader, Novi Michigan

BASIC STEPS OF A TYPICAL PBL PROJECT

Launch	The teacher defines (often with input from students) an engaging, challenging problem or complex question for students to investigate.
Investigation	Students learn the knowledge and skills needed to address the problem or question. The teacher provides resources and lessons. The students may talk with experts from outside the classroom.
Creation	Students develop their solution to the problem or answer to the question. They often create a physical object, a display, a media product, or an event.
Demonstration	Students share their work publicly, with people beyond their classroom.

Projects in school have been around for a long time, but not all "projects" result in important learning and skill development. Today, when done well, the projects in PBL are much more in-depth and complex than many projects were in the past.

Some projects are "dessert"—but PBL makes the project the "main course." For example, you might have seen "dessert" projects like these:

- Build a model of something.
- Make a diorama or map.
- Create a poster or display.
- Research a topic and make a presentation.

Dessert projects are appropriate in some situations, but they do not teach as much as "main course" projects. A main course project is not something a teacher assigns alongside or at the end of a traditional unit of instruction. Instead, the project is the unit. The project is the vehicle for teaching the important knowledge and skills students need to learn.

Dessert Project: Build a motorized Mars rover vehicle using Legos.

VS.

Main Course Project (PBL): Work with a NASA scientist to help plan a trip to Mars. Do research and use maps to learn about the surface of Mars. (And also build a Lego vehicle!)

WHY AND HOW PBL IS USED

Why is PBL becoming more popular in education?

Today's Economy: Educators understand that to be successful on the job and in a career in today's economy, people need to have more than basic knowledge and skills. Recent state education standards ask students to think critically, solve real-life problems, collaborate with others, and communicate their ideas. PBL teaches these skills better than traditional instructional methods.

Technology: The increasing use of technology in education has made it easier for students to do research, work together, create things, and just as important, connect the classroom with the outside world.

Teachers and students like it: Teachers are finding it enjoyable and rewarding to use a teaching method that, when done well, excites students and gives them valuable skills.

-- Devin, 11th grader, San Francisco

BENEFITS OF USING PBL

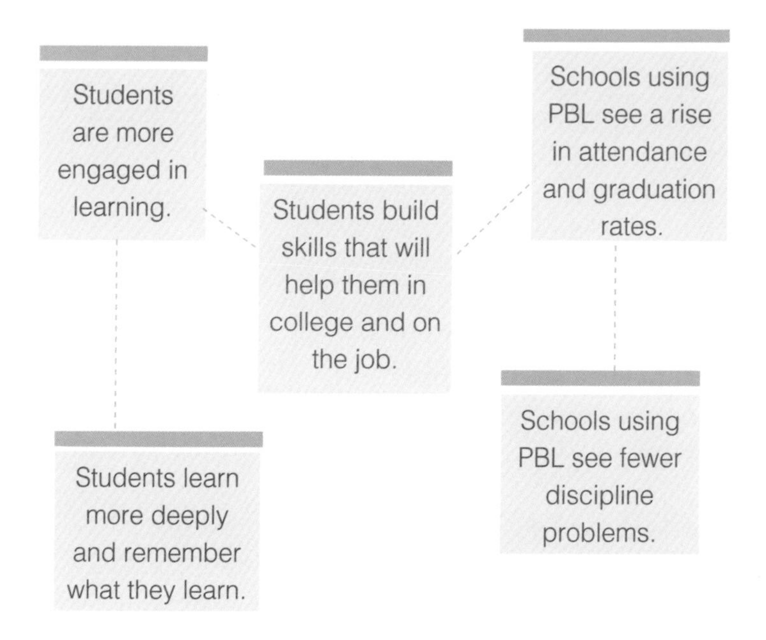

Are we talking about using PBL in "regular" classes, or just in special programs?

Some schools have popular programs such as "maker spaces" or "genius hours" in which students do projects for an hour or two a week. Some high schools require students to complete independent research projects or service-learning projects, often in their senior year. These programs are great, but PBL has a more powerful effect on students when it's used more often. Teachers can teach "regular" subjects very effectively with PBL.

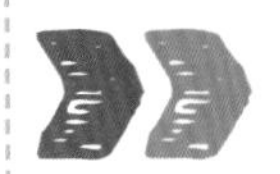

TO SEE EXAMPLES OF PROJECTS FOR DIFFERENT GRADE LEVELS AND A VARIETY OF SUBJECTS, SEE PAGE 33.

IS PBL APPROPRIATE FOR...

All grade levels?

PBL works for students in kindergarten and all the way up through high school, college, and graduate school. Teachers can design and manage the projects so that they meet the needs of their specific students.

All subject areas?

Projects can be designed to teach any subject. Middle school or high school teachers of some subject areas, such as math, literature, or world languages, might choose to do fewer projects or design them differently compared to other subjects. Many projects will combine more than one subject, as the ones on page one and two do, because many real-life problems and issues are complex.

-- Becky, parent of 2nd grader, Walnut Creek, CA

Advanced Placement (AP) courses?
The College Board's Advanced Placement program has recently been changing the requirements for AP courses in ways that are PBL-friendly. Research has shown that students taught with PBL do better on AP tests than students taught using traditional methods that emphasize simply "covering" huge amounts of material.

CHALLENGES OF USING PBL FOR FIRST TIME USERS

Students, teachers, and schools may encounter the following challenges when they first begin using PBL (fortunately, these issues fade away over time as they get more experienced):

- **Students** who are used to traditional teaching may take awhile to adjust to PBL and may need to be taught how to work on projects.
- **Teachers** who are comfortable with traditional teaching methods may find they need to learn additional skills for PBL and adopt some new ways of thinking about what and how students should learn.
- **Schools** organized for traditional teaching and learning will find they need to make some changes in order to support the use of PBL. Administrators will want to support teachers and manage these changes carefully.

"WE HAVE BEEN BLOWN AWAY BY THE PASSION, CREATIVITY, DEPTH AND COMMITMENT SHE AND HER GROUP MEMBERS HAVE SHOWN."

-- JANET, PARENT OF HIGH SCHOOL STUDENT, SAUSALITO, CA

STUDENTS AND PBL

What do students learn with PBL?
In a good project, students still learn a lot of "the basics." They learn how to apply reading, writing, and math skills. They gain knowledge of science, history, and other subjects, and at the same time they also gain a deeper understanding of concepts and issues.

Projects also build those skills described earlier that will help students succeed on the job and in further education: how to solve real-life problems, find resources, work in teams, and make presentations.

Students who successfully complete projects also learn valuable things about themselves. They become empowered. They know they can take on challenges, work hard over a period of time, and create high-quality work. Many projects also give students experience in the world outside school, and point them toward careers or lifelong interests.

Do students do projects all the time when teachers use PBL?
Some PBL teachers use projects as their regular teaching method, but many switch PBL up with other activities. Some teachers may do several projects a year, while others may do just two or three.

Do students still do homework during projects?

Students still do homework in PBL, but it may look different from the assignments parents are used to. For example, instead of reading textbooks or doing worksheets, students may spend several days doing research on the Internet. They may create or build something that takes time on a weekend. They may plan and practice a presentation they will be making. They may communicate online with other students to plan their work. (Schools and teachers using PBL provide support and guidance for parents of students working on projects.)

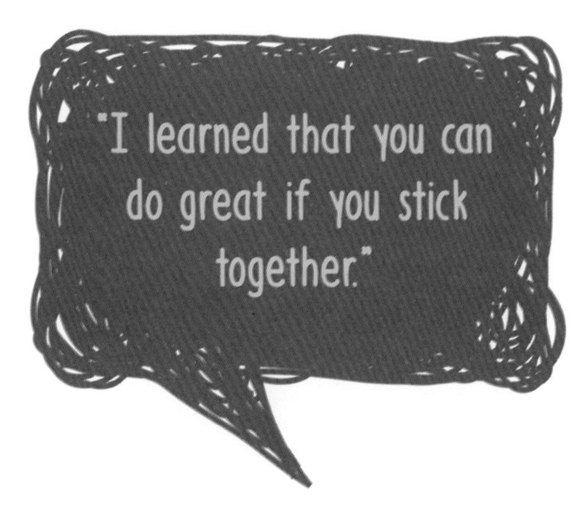

-- Alanna, 3rd grader, reflecting on a project, Saluda, SC

IS PBL EFFECTIVE FOR ALL STUDENTS?

PBL benefits all students because they:

- do more challenging and meaningful work
- explore their own interests and share their talents
- see how learning connects to real life
- build skills in critical thinking, problem-solving, communication, and creativity/innovation
- learn how to manage time well, work independently, and meet deadlines (project management skills)
- learn how to work on an effective team
- feel that they can make a difference in the world
- are exposed to the world of work and career possibilities

-- Mia, 6th grader, San Jose, CA

IS PBL APPROPRIATE FOR...

Students who are English learners?

Projects give students a chance to talk with and listen to other students as they work together in a team, and also to interact with adults in real-life situations. Projects also allow students to draw on their strengths and skills and share those with classmates. English language development goals can easily be included in project requirements.

Students with disabilities?

Students with disabilities feel included in projects done with their peers and can lend their skills and talents to the team. Compared to focusing on whole-class instruction, teachers are more able to provide additional support to individual students during project work time.

Students who are gifted and talented?

Compared with many traditional assignments, projects can give students a real challenge. Every project is different, so students have to solve new problems and learn to work with a variety of people. Students can put their special talents to good use in projects involving music, drama, technology, art, or hands-on work.

COMMON CONCERNS ABOUT GROUP WORK

When students work in teams, don't some students do more or less than their fair share of the work?
Students who are not used to working in teams may not know how, at first. Some students may want to "take over" the team. Others may want to sit back and wait for everyone else to do the work. But when a teacher manages a project well and teaches students how to work in a team, they do their fair share of the work. The culture of the PBL classroom should look like that of a healthy, well-functioning workplace where people share the load.

What about students who don't like to work in a group?
Working with others can be challenging for some students, but PBL teachers know how to build the skills and classroom culture that make it easier. Many things in school that challenge students—like learning fractions—are valuable for their lives. Being able to work well with others is valuable, too.

Are students' grades for a project based only on the work done by the team?
Grades related to a project should be based mainly on an individual student's work, not on what is created by the team. Projects should include individual assignments on which grades can be based. Also, PBL teachers know how to identify what each student contributed to a team effort, and this helps them to give grades fairly.

THE RESEARCH ON PBL

THERE IS RESEARCH TO SUPPORT THE STATEMENTS IN THE PREVIOUS SECTION ABOUT HOW PBL IS EFFECTIVE FOR VARIOUS TYPES OF STUDENTS AND FOR VARIOUS SUBJECT AREAS. HERE ARE SOME MORE THINGS RESEARCHERS HAVE FOUND ABOUT PBL.

RESEARCH HAS SHOWN PBL IMPROVES STUDENT LEARNING BECAUSE IT:

- improves student motivation
- builds critical thinking and problem solving skills
- increases students' understanding of concepts and their ability to apply knowledge in real-life situations
- helps students to remember what they have learned longer and to use that knowledge in new situations

BESIDES IMPROVING LEARNING, RESEARCH HAS SHOWN THAT:

- in PBL classrooms, students have a better attitude toward learning
- PBL shows promise for closing the achievement gap by engaging lower-achieving students
- teachers who use PBL show increased job satisfaction

How does PBL affect standardized test scores?
Projects should be designed to include the important knowledge and skills measured by tests. Studies have shown that, when projects are well designed, the use of PBL at a school can improve scores on tests. Students who learn material through Project Based Learning remember it better when test-taking time arrives. Also, many tests today are beginning to measure skills like critical thinking and problem-solving, and PBL is an effective way to learn these skills.

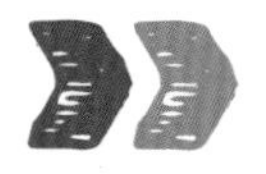

FOR MORE INFORMATION FROM THE RESEARCH ON PBL, VISIT WWW.BIE.ORG/OBJECTS/CAT/RESEARCH

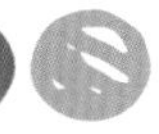

"PBL HAS GIVEN ME A SENSE OF PURPOSE BECAUSE THE PROJECTS THAT YOU UNDERTAKE HAVE A DIRECT EFFECT ON YOUR FRIENDS AND SOMETIMES EVEN YOUR COMMUNITY."

-- CALEB, 9TH GRADER, COLUMBUS, IN

PART THREE: WHAT CAN YOU EXPECT AT A SCHOOL THAT USES PROJECT BASED LEARNING?

A SCHOOL THAT HAS DECIDED TO USE PROJECT BASED LEARNING AS A TEACHING METHOD WILL BE DIFFERENT FROM A "REGULAR" SCHOOL. HERE'S WHAT YOU CAN EXPECT TO SEE:

Students who are more excited about school.
When kids come home from school and parents ask, "What did you do at school today?" the answer is often "nothing." With PBL, the answer is usually different. Students will talk about their project work and show pride in what they have done. When you walk onto the campus of a school using PBL, you can often feel the energy and excitement.

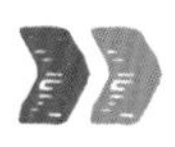

A school and classrooms that look and feel different.
When you visit a PBL school, you will notice students' work from projects displayed on the walls and sense a lively energy. When you walk by a PBL classroom, it will be active and maybe even a bit noisy when students are engaged in project work.

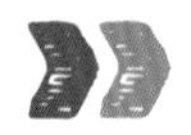

Different uses of classroom time.

Some of the time in a PBL classroom, students will be working in teams. They may be going to the library/media center or off campus. They may also be using computers, phones, and tablets to do research, to create things, or to communicate with experts outside the classroom. They may be sharing work with each other for feedback, creating a list of questions to investigate, and preparing presentations.

Longer class periods in middle and high school, and flexible use of time in elementary school.

Work on a project proceeds more effectively when students have a class period longer than 45 minutes. Many middle and high schools using PBL have created 75- to 90-minute periods. Sometimes they also combine two classes, such as English and social studies, for project work. In elementary schools, students may work on a project for part of a day, or much of the day, or only on certain days.

More connections to the world outside the classroom.

Students learning through PBL often make contact with adults at school besides their teachers, and also with community members, experts on particular topics, and people and organizations across town or around the world.

In addition, local business owners or people who work in a local industry may be asked to speak with teachers about ideas for real-life projects. They might act as a "client" for students who are "consultants" doing a project. They could be asked to be an expert advisor to students, to help evaluate students' work, or to be the audience for presentations.

Options for parent/family involvement in projects.

With PBL, parents have an opportunity to be more involved in their child's education. If students are excited by a project, parents are likely to hear about it and can help their children think about it. Parents will be able to use their skills and experience to help their children with projects, and will be invited to join the audience when students present their work.

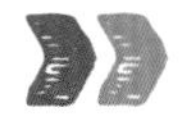

Public exhibitions of student work.
Since a big part of PBL is making students' work public, many schools invite parents and the community to come and see it. For example, instead of the usual Open House in the spring, some PBL schools are having an Exhibition Night, when students share projects with parents and the community.

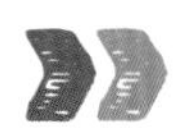

More planning time for teachers.
PBL functions better when teachers can work with each other in planning projects and thinking about ways to improve them. Many schools using PBL have a shorter school day once a week to give teachers time to meet. Teachers often spend time in the summer planning projects.

-- kindergartener at project exhibition night, Nashville, TN

Fewer problems with student behavior and better attendance.

When students are engaged in project work that matters to them, they are less likely to be causing trouble. They are also more likely to want to attend school.

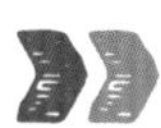

Support for teachers from administrators.

The school principal, vice principal, other school staff, and district staff and administrators all contribute to the success of PBL in classrooms. They can help teachers to learn about PBL and to work together to improve the school's use of PBL. They can create new schedules, provide equipment and other resources, and make community connections to support PBL. They can seek the funding needed for teacher training, and also for upgrading technology, since good Internet access makes PBL easier for teachers and students.

"KIDS COME HOME EXCITED ABOUT SCHOOL. IT'S REALLY GREAT WATCHING THEM HAVE FUN WITH LEARNING."
-- JENIFER, PARENT OF 5TH GRADER EXPERIENCING PBL, EUGENE, OR

PROJECT EXAMPLES

HERE ARE SOME EXAMPLES OF HIGH-QUALITY PBL PROJECTS THAT HAVE BEEN DONE AT DIFFERENT GRADE LEVELS AND IN A VARIETY OF SUBJECTS.

ELEMENTARY SCHOOL:

Kindergarten

Students create an illustrated book about the life cycles of local wild animals, to be displayed at their county's Conservation District office.

First Grade

Students test various ways to solve the problem of conflict around their school campus by making posters, writing signed community agreements, and raising awareness of issues such as teasing and not sharing.

Second Grade

Students partner with local organizations to fill a need in their community or beyond it, such as collecting toys for sick children, food for the homeless, supplies for victims of a natural disaster, or creating promotional materials for an environmental clean-up, healthy eating campaign, or animal adoption event.

Third Grade

Students interview older community residents and work with a local museum to learn about their town's history. create podcasts and host a "Community History Day" event with presentations and displays.

Fourth Grade

Students design and implement a plan to improve their school campus by creating insect habitats, providing nesting sites for birds, planting native plants, or removing weeds and invasive plants.

Fifth Grade

Students use math to determine the best mobile phone plan for themselves and their families, visiting websites and contacting representatives of phone service providers for information. They present their recommendations to an audience of parents and middle school students, and post a "guide to cell phone plans" on their school website.

MIDDLE SCHOOL:

Math

Students find out how much a pizza chain restaurant is really charging when customers pay for each topping, and decide whether its prices, based on the number of toppings, are fair and competitive.

Science

Students design and conduct a scientific experiment to test claims by a company that aeroponic growing methods (using only nutrient-enriched water) can produce more food and use less land and water compared to traditional soil-based growing methods. They communicate their results in a written report and video conference presentation to a representative of the company.

Math and Science

Students design proposals for a new restaurant for their community, working with an architect and presenting their plans to community members and representatives of the city government.

History

Students plan and conduct a role-play "trial" of U.S. President Truman, to decide whether it was right to drop the atomic bomb on Japan during World War II.

Spanish Language and Graphic Design

Students create signs for a local business to put on the wall, with messages in Spanish about workplace procedures.

English and Social Studies

Students read a novel about a person who was a hero, then identify "local heroes" in their community to interview. They publish a book of photos and written reflections about their heroes.

Science, Technology, Engineering, Art, and Math

Students create their own 3D model of an artificial island, like the Palm Islands in Dubai, along with an advertisement and a marketing plan to sell the homes on their island.

English, Social Studies, Math, and Business

Students come up with ideas for new products and services and develop a business plan, which they pitch to experts from finance, engineering, and other fields at a young entrepreneurs event. Or they might even create and run their own business.

HIGH SCHOOL:

Math

Students use geometry to design holes for a miniature golf course, acting as consultants to a local business owner who wants to attract more customers.

Science

Students use knowledge of chemistry to make hard-tack candy, which they sell in a school fundraiser.

Technology, Engineering and Math

Students design, build, and program remote-controlled toy vehicles and run them through various tests and races.

Economics, Civics, Math, and English

Students propose ideas for redevelopment of an area in their city, creating scale models and working with experts from the planning commission.

English

Students publish a book of nonfiction writing in which they tell family stories of growing up and coming of age.

Social Studies and Science

Students create music videos for the United Way website about infant health and brain development, and other issues affecting children in their community.

English, Social Studies, Art and Technology

Students analyze state election propositions, then create videos and written materials to persuade voters, which they present to an audience of parents and community members.

Career and Technical Education

Students work in teams to design and manufacture a metal stool within a given budget. They research stools from online vendors and interview local mechanics, who test their designs and give students feedback.

History and Art

Students investigate the question, "Why do people immigrate and how has immigration changed our community?" and work with local artists to create a mural on a public building that expresses their answer, in addition to writing.

Science, Art, Civics, English, and Technology

Students learn where and how their food is grown locally, visit farmers, and create "pop-up" art show displays using photographs and writing to educate their community. They also make presentations to local government agencies about issues related to agriculture.

World Languages

Students who are novices in a language create an illustrated story about life in another country; advanced students create a film in another language about an American exchange student's life in high school in another country.

VIDEOS & WEBSITES ABOUT PROJECT BASED LEARNING

VIDEOS ONLINE

Project Based Learning: Explained
What PBL is and how it builds skills for 21st-century success.
(animated, 4 minutes)
http://bie.org/x6Pb

"It really, actually changed my life"
High school students talk about what they gain from PBL.
(4 minutes)
http://bie.org/x4Ub

Keep It Real
The author of the book *Hip Hop Genius* explains the importance of real-life PBL.
(3 1/2 minutes)
http://bie.org/x66k

Elementary Projects From Worms to Wall Street
A look at various elementary school projects.
(7 minutes)
http://bie.org/x4ge

Middle School Project: Public Art

How students learned about local history as they created models and wrote proposals for installing works of art around their city.
(7 minutes)
http://bie.org/x7re

High School Project: Media Saves the Beach

How students learned science and used writing and technology skills in a project involving civic participation to clean up local beaches.
(5 1/2 minutes)
http://bie.org/x2se

WEBSITES

BUCK INSTITUTE FOR EDUCATION:

BIE.ORG

EDUTOPIA:

EDUTOPIA.ORG

PARTNERSHIP FOR 21ST CENTURY LEARNING:

P21.ORG

DEEPER LEARNING:

DEEPERLEARNING4ALL.ORG/ABOUT-DEEPER-LEARNING